BRITAIN IN OLD PH

RICKMANSW
CHORLEYWOOD &
CROXLEY GREEN

EDMUND PARROTT

ALAN SUTTON PUBLISHING LIMITED

Alan Sutton Publishing Limited
Phoenix Mill · Far Thrupp · Stroud
Gloucestershire · GL5 2BU

First published 1996

Cover photographs: front: Church Street on coronation day, 1902. The decorations are out and the people are dressed in their best clothes for the occasion; back: a group photograph taken at the Rickmansworth Cricket Club, when the club-house was first opened in 1924.

British Library Cataloguing in Publication Data
A catalogue record for this book is available from the British Library.

ISBN 0-7509-1086-0

Typeset in 10/12 Perpetua.
Typesetting and origination by Alan Sutton Publishing Limited.
Printed in Great Britain by Ebenezer Baylis, Worcester.

Batchworth, 1910. The iron bridge was constructed in 1833. On the right is the original White Bear public house.

CONTENTS

The water splash in Bury Lane was once one of the best-known beauty spots in Rickmansworth. The road was originally a private drive to the Bury Manor House, but in the early eighteenth century the lord of the manor gave permission for it to be used by the public, on condition that the townspeople built and maintained a footbridge over the stream. This view, taken in the early 1900s, presents a peaceful rural scene. The gates to the Bury can be seen in the distance. Motor vehicles driving through the stream during the very bad winter of 1962/3 caused a build-up of ice on the road coming out of it and the road had to be closed on a number of occasions. As a result, in the autumn of 1963, the council culverted the stream, removed the footbridge and made up the road.

INTRODUCTION

Man lived in this locale long before it had a name. The evidence of worked flints and bones indicates human presence between the various ice ages that laid down the gravel beds for which this area is well known. Some of the finds from the earliest Stone Age period were made at the beginning of this century in the dry gravel pits at Mill End and Croxley Green. Since then many other discoveries have been made in the pits which now form the lakes that stretch from Tolpits Lane to West Hyde. Prehistoric animal remains have also been found, including elephant and mammoth tusks, bones of other animals, and antlers of giant red deer. Worked flints from the later Stone Age have been found all over this area, and continue to turn up regularly in the gardens and freshly ploughed fields.

Evidence of occupation during the Bronze Age (c. 1800 BC) has been found in the Chess Valley and in 1949 a hoard of axe heads, ingots and other pieces of bronze was found in The Drive, Rickmansworth. A similar hoard from the same period has also been found in Tolpits Lane, Watford. During the construction of the M25 motorway traces of Iron Age settlement were found in Berry Lane Woods. The finds included pottery that has been dated definitely to the sixth or seventh century BC.

By the first century BC this area had become part of the nation of the Catuvellauni, a tribe of ancient Britons who fought against the first invasions of the Romans under Julius Caesar in 55 BC and 54 BC. It is recorded that Caesar's legions came up the Thames Valley to Brentford, and then to Wheathampstead. It is therefore possible, as some researchers believe, that their route took them through the Colne Valley. After the successful invasion of AD 43 this area certainly proved to be attractive to them for settlement, and villas are to be found in the Chess Valley at Latimer and Sarratt, and in the Colne Valley at Moor Park and Sandy Lodge. Traces of a Roman water mill have been found at Loudwater.

Little is known about this area in the so-called Dark Ages, following the breakdown of the central Roman government in the fifth century. However, by the middle of the eighth century it was part of the Anglo-Saxon kingdom of Mercia, under the rule of King Offa. King Offa founded the abbey at St Albans, and when he died in AD 796 his son Ecgfrid came to the throne; in order to bring blessings on his kingdom, he granted the Manor of Pynnelsfeld West Hyde and five farmsteads to the abbey.

It was during this period that the Saxons divided the country into shires, and it was probably at about this time that the first settlement began to develop in what is now the town centre. The name Rickmansworth is derived from Ryckmer, a personal Saxon name, and worth, the Saxon word for a farm.

There was certainly a settlement here by the time of the Norman invasion in 1066. Rickmansworth was listed as Prichemaresworde in the Doomsday survey of 1086. There was no mention of a church in this survey, but there is a record of a chaplain in the manor in 1119. In 1219 Pope Honorius III confirmed the grant of a church at Rickmansworth to the abbey at St Albans. The present St Mary's Church dates from 1890. It replaced an earlier building of 1826, which had in turn replaced the earlier church which stood on the site. The tower had been restored in 1630 and survived both the later rebuildings. The town continued to grow under the Norman kings, and it seems that some time between 1216 and 1227 Henry III gave the town its first charter. It was, however, definitely given a charter and the right to hold a market by Henry VIII in 1542.

From Saxon times until the end of the sixteenth century local government had been manorial, with the lord of the manor being responsible for enforcing laws and collecting taxes. Acts of Parliament passed in 1598 and 1601 transferred the powers of the lord of the manor to the Vestry, and later Acts gave the Vestry even more powers. During the eighteenth and nineteenth centuries there were steep rises in poor rate demands, which led to various Acts of Parliament being passed which started the breakdown of the Vestry system. In Rickmansworth it finally came to an end in 1894 when the town opted for parish council status. The first meeting of the new body for the election of members was held on 4 December 1894.

In 1895 it was resolved that an urban district council be appointed in the parish of Rickmansworth, but it was not until 6 April 1898 that a meeting was held to elect members to the new authority. It was at this time that the Chorleywood representatives decided to opt for separate parish council status, and thus Chorleywood became a separate rural district council; it became an urban district in 1935. Croxley Green remained part of Rickmansworth. In April 1974 Chorleywood and Rickmansworth were reunited under the local government reorganization, and together with Abbots Langley, Sarratt, and Oxhey they now form the Three Rivers District.

Transport has played a considerable part in the development of the area from the eighteenth century onwards, with the building of two turnpike roads, the canal in 1796, the first railway in 1862, the 'Met' railway in 1887 and finally the M25 motorway in 1976. The turnpike roads were the Hatfield to Reading Trust, which ran through Croxley Green, Rickmansworth and Chorleywood, and the Pinner Trust which ran from the bottom of Batchworth Hill to Pinner.

Following the construction of the Grand Junction Canal in 1796, several small branches were built from it. The biggest and most important of these led off from the second lock at Batchworth and went to Salter's Brewery at the east end of the High Street. The branch was in use by 1805 and when the Rickmansworth Gas Company opened in 1852, it was used by them to bring in coal; this explains why it is still referred to by many people as 'The Gasworks Arm'.

The first railway in Rickmansworth ran from Watford High Street to Church Street and was opened in 1862. It was closed to passenger traffic in 1952 and to goods traffic a few years later. The station was demolished in 1973. The Metropolitan Line was extended to Rickmansworth in 1887, and a few years later was carried on through Chorleywood to Aylesbury. In 1925 the line was electrified from Baker Street as far as Rickmansworth, but since the trains still ran through to Aylesbury, this meant that the engines had to be changed at Rickmansworth from electric to steam coming from London, and vice versa. This practice was brought to an end on 9 September 1961, when the line was electrified through to Amersham, which then became its terminal.

The modern road works which have had such a dramatic effect on the appearance of this area began in the 1930s when the bypass from the station to Park Road was opened and the bridges over the canal and the rivers in Church Street were rebuilt. Road building continued with the construction of the dual carriageway in Rectory Road during the late 1950s and early 1960s, the building of the Ebury and Station roundabouts, Riverside Drive and Batchworth roundabout in Rickmansworth, and the Baldwins Lane roundabout and dual carriageway over the canal and river in Croxley Green. In 1972 Scots Hill, which had always been a source of major hold-ups and fatal accidents, was finally made into a dual carriageway.

For all this time, from as early as the 1930s, the arguments raged for and against the construction of the North Orbital Road from Maple Cross to Hunton Bridge. The people of Rickmansworth and Croxley Green wanted it, but those living in Chorleywood were against it. The matter was finally settled in 1973 and work on the road started. It was opened on 26 February 1976 as an ordinary bypass road but has since become the M25 motorway; plans to widen it are still causing arguments in the 1990s.

The residential development of the area began in earnest in the early 1920s when the council started building houses at Grove Road and Springwell Avenue in Mill End, and at Springwell Close in Croxley Green. Private developments started at the same time in Moor Park and Loudwater, followed by more at Croxley Green and the Cedars Estate. The Money Hill shopping centre was started on the north side of Uxbridge Road in 1928.

Since the war considerable residential development has taken place with large council estates at Berry Lane and Maple Cross, and many other smaller council and private developments scattered all over the area. As a result of all this building, the population has risen from about 8,000 in 1920 to about 30,000 in the late 1990s for Rickmansworth, with approximately 80,000 in the whole of the Three Rivers area. During the 1960s a number of historic buildings in the town centre were demolished, but in spite of this the town still retains some of the charm of a small market town, and is a pleasant place to live in or visit.

THE TOWN CENTRE

In May 1900 the town was decorated to celebrate the relief of Mafeking in the South African war. This was the scene in the High Street; the Swan Hotel is on the right.

The Old Market Hall on its site behind the High Street. It was erected there in 1804 after the original hall was removed from the centre of the High Street. By the 1860s it had deteriorated because of disuse into this dilapidated state and was photographed by Mr J. Croft in 1868 shortly before it was demolished. The site today is occupied by the brick-built town hall which replaced it and which is now used as an office.

Price's newsagents shop in Station Road, 1902. The shop was started about 1890 and continued to trade under the same name until the 1970s.

The High Street in 1872, photographed by J. Croft. The Fotherley Almshouses and Station Road are on the right. Note the unmade-up road, and the haystack in what is now the west end of the High Street.

This is one of the most common views of the High Street. The date of this photograph is unknown, but it would appear to be the early 1900s as there is not a car to be seen, and the town hall on the left is still a hall – in 1912 it was converted into the town's first cinema. The Swan Hotel is on the right.

The Fotherley Almshouses, 1912. They were built in the High Street in 1682 by John Fotherley for 'five poor widows', each of whom lived in one room. The almshouses were demolished in the early 1930s and replaced by the present building which is today occupied by Mackays. The stone plaque shown above the door in this photograph can still be seen today, set high in the wall of the present building.

The High Street, 1902. The Fotherley Almshouses are on the left while on the right stands the recently constructed Westminster Bank building. Note the empty space next door and the buildings opposite which are still there today with their ground floors converted to shops.

The Swan Hotel, 1912. Perhaps one of the people shown was Mr L.T. Simmonds, the landlord at that time.

The Swan Hotel in 1964, shortly before it closed. The main building has changed very little from the earlier photographs.

The Swan plaque was removed from the building on 11 October 1964. It was made of Coade stone and can be seen today in the Three Rivers Museum. In the photograph are Mr E. Parrott and his sons Leslie and Melvyn; they were helped by Mr L. Leach and the author.

Station Road in 1963, shortly before everything on this side of the road was demolished for the construction of Penn Place. The first building on the right was the Tree restaurant, named after the tree which can be seen here breaking the wall.

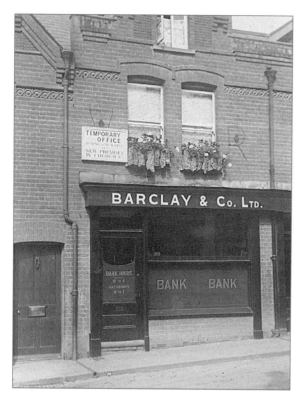

The temporary premises occupied by Barclays Bank in Station Road in 1902 while their present building was under construction in Church Street.

Church Street, looking towards the High Street, during mains drainage works in 1902. On the far left is the site of Barclays Bank, with a sign giving information about its construction.

The High Street, looking towards the west end, during mains drainage works in 1902. The Foresters Arms public house stood on the corner of Station Road.

This peaceful scene on the corner of the High Street and Station Road dates from 1902.

The end of the row of early seventeenth-century cottages on the corner of Talbot Road and the High Street. This photograph was taken in 1963, shortly before they were demolished.

Looking up Station Road during the laying of the mains drainage in the town in 1902.

G. Jones was first established as a coachbuilder in
the 1800s at these premises in Church Street.
The date of this photograph is not known but
since the advertisement mentions cars it is
probably early in the 1900s.

The Bell Inn in the High Street, 1904. Built in about 1600, it was one of the oldest buildings in the town.
It closed as a pub in 1912, and from then until its demolition in 1967 it served as the offices of Swannell
and Sly. The public library stands on the site today.

Rickmansworth's first public library. Situated behind Basing House, it was opened in 1943 as a 'temporary' building, but continued to serve the town until May 1968 when the present library was opened.

This photograph of Penn Place was taken in 1964, shortly after the precinct was opened, and was produced as a colour postcard for publicity purposes.

Soloman's Hill, 1963. This back road led from the High Street to the back of the shops, and the houses on the hill. It was photographed during the demolitions prior to the construction of Penn Place. The section of footpath next to Boots shop is still called Solomans Hill today.

This view of the High Street was taken in 1936 when the buildings next to Boots were being demolished. The present shops on the site were built at that time.

Church Street, 1900. Bury Lane is on the left. Note the meat hanging outside the butcher's shop, and the dogs sniffing around below it.

Talbot Road, looking towards the High Street, c. 1900. The Methodist church and the cottages at the far end were demolished in the 1980s.

A London North Western Railway dray delivering to one of the shops in the High Street in 1911.

The fish and chip shop on the corner of Bury Lane and Church Street in the early 1900s. The shop closed in the 1980s and the building is now an office.

These two views of the High Street in 1937 show the coronation decorations. At this time traffic travelled in both directions. The one-way system was started in 1962, and is still in force today. This year, 1996, the High Street underwent a major refurbishment, with traffic still allowed through, but with much wider pavements and pedestrian areas.

This photograph, taken in the garden of The Priory in Church Street in 1930, is reputed to show a Roman bath. However, it is more likely to be a replica built by the eccentric Mr Leftwhich who lived there at that time. The garden also contained a Chinese pagoda and various other objects from all around the world.

Church Street on coronation day, 1902. The decorations are out and the people are dressed in their best clothes for the occasion.

The east end of the High Street, 1910. On the left is the Coach and Horses public house and on the right the Wesleyan chapel. Built and consecrated in 1866, the chapel was in regular use until the early 1980s when the site was sold. The chapel itself was demolished in 1984 and an office built on the site. The white building and some of the cottages are still recognizable today.

The site of the Odeon cinema in 1965, looking towards the High Street. The buildings in the High Street are (left to right), the end of Swannell and Slys, a private house and the old gas company showroom.

The site of the Odeon cinema in 1965, looking towards Talbot Road. The warehouse on the left was demolished in the 1970s. The other buildings were Beeson's shops. They were demolished in the late 1980s and replaced with offices of a very similar design.

This cottage stands at the west end of the High Street and its ground floor has been converted into a shop, currently called Present Trends. The lady in the doorway is believed to be a member of the Boston family, photographed in around 1905.

Station Road, 1890. At this time it was called Keepers Hill. All the buildings shown here were demolished shortly after this photograph was taken and the buildings which replaced them were in turn demolished in 1995, to make way for the new buildings which are now on the site.

AROUND THE TOWN

The town's first swimming pool was situated in Ebury Road on land given to the town by Lord Ebury. It was officially opened in 1909 by Lord Ebury himself. It is remembered by many people primarily because it was always so cold: it had no heating and was fed by the freshwater stream alongside it. It was closed in the 1970s and the flats in Goral Mead now stand on its site.

Rickmansworth's war memorial originally stood on the corner of Ebury Road and Uxbridge Road. It had to be moved in 1968 because it was in the way of new road works. This caused considerable controversy when it was decided to put the memorial in the churchyard but without the statue of the lion and the eagle on the top, because the statue was not of a religious nature. The memorial itself can still be seen in the churchyard. The arguments over the lion and the eagle went on for over ten years, but today it can be seen on a separate plinth in the council rose gardens at Three Rivers House.

Rickmansworth Park House was built in 1740 by Henry Fotherley-Whitfield, Lord of the Manor of Rickmansworth. This postcard view from the 1920s actually shows the side and back of the house – the large portico was *not* at the front, and the real front door was on the other side of the house.

The portico on the side of the house was a late addition to the original building. The people shown are Mr and Mrs Lane who lived in the empty house as caretakers between 1924 and 1926 when it was demolished. The Masonic School stands on the site today.

In May 1960 Rickmansworth UDC purchased the Aquadrome, which included Bury Lake and the grounds around it. One of their first acts was to replace the footbridge over the River Colne which led from the recreation ground to Bury Lake. This photograph shows the new bridge being put in place, with the old bridge on the left. The old bridge's foundations were not very stable and it swayed as people crossed it; its steep steps were also a problem.

This postcard of the old footbridge over the River Colne was produced in the 1920s. The footbridge was erected in 1914, when the Walker Brothers opened the grounds and Bury lake to the public.

The rear of the Old Vicarage in Bury Lane, photographed from the back garden. Part of the front of this house is the oldest building in Rickmansworth and dates from the fifteenth century; it can be seen through the open gateway in Church Street. The building is now used as offices.

The Bury was built in the mid-seventeenth century by Sir Gilbert Wakering who had been granted the lease of the site from the crown. This view of the west front was taken in the 1920s. Today the house is owned by the County Council and is standing empty, although most of the grounds are now a public recreation amenity.

The gates of the Bury facing Bury Lane were demolished in the 1930s.

This postcard of the Bury gardens also dates from the 1920s. The stream still runs through the grounds today.

The old bridge over the canal leading to the Aquadrome. The centre section of this bridge was removed in 1940 as part of the defensive ring around London. It was replaced by the present bridge after the war.

The Halfway House in Uxbridge Road, 1907. This is still a very popular pub today.

The hamlet of Two Stones on the Uxbridge Road, 1907. On the far right is Halfway House. The cottages shown here were demolished in 1912 and replaced by very similar houses which are still there today.

Parsonage Farm is one of the oldest farmhouses in the area and dates from the sixteenth century. It is constructed of the narrow bricks of the period.

Parsonage Farm in the 1960s. A chimney stack has been removed and it has had a general facelift but it is still largely the same as in the previous photograph. The house is still there today, but is now surrounded by new houses.

Rickmansworth Park in the 1920s looking towards Park House, which is just visible in the centre of the picture. A few of the trees are still standing.

Looking up Nightingale Road to open fields at the top end, in the 1900s.

CROXLEY GREEN

Croxley windmill, early 1950s. This tower mill was built in 1820 and served the area as a corn mill until the 1880s when a storm carried away the sails and damaged the cap. After that it was used for various purposes until the 1950s when it was converted into a house and had an extention built onto it. It still survives today in the centre of the Windmill Estate at the top of Scots Hill.

The tithe barn at Croxley Hall Farm is one of the oldest and largest barns in the country. It was built in about 1420 for the abbey at St Albans. During the 1950s its condition started to deteriorate through lack of use, but the owners could not afford to repair it. By the early 1970s it had reached the state shown above, but soon afterwards it was purchased by the county council as part of the enlargement of St Joan of Arc school, which meant that it could be repaired as a school building. The repairs took place in 1973 and the building is now in the condition shown below.

Croxley Mill, showing the 'Egyptian Front'. Lord Ebury only allowed the mill to be built on common land on condition that it did not spoil his view, and so the 'Egyptian front' was built facing Moor Park Mansion.

A works outing from Dickinsons mill at Croxley Green in 1919.

All Saint's Church and the Green at Croxley. This photograph pre-dates 1912 when an extension was added to the church.

New Road at the corner of Dickinson Square, 1910. The occasion is not known but the children appear to be dressed in their best clothes.

The almshouses which stood on the corner of the Green and Scots Hill, 1903. Officially called Berean Cottages, they were known as 'Penny Row' as this was the weekly rent when they were first built. They were demolished in 1932 when the present church hall was built on the site.

The view at the top of Scots Hill, looking towards the church in the early 1900s. The hall and cottages on the far right were destroyed by a bomb on 19 February 1943 and most of the buildings on the left were demolished in the 1960s.

The well-head mechanism and shelter at Croxley House on its original site just outside the back door. It was constructed in the late eighteenth century over a well that was more than 90 ft deep. In the mid-1970s the structure was in the way of extensions to the house, so it was moved to the rear lawn where it can still be seen today.

Looking up Scots Hill in 1971, shortly before the road was made into a dual carriageway. This road is now the 'down' carriageway only.

CHORLEYWOOD

A peaceful scene in Heronsgate Road, the Swillett, in the early 1920s. The shops are just out of sight on the right. The road has since been widened but the house shown is still there today.

The seventeenth-century Kings Farm, 1900. Here William Penn married Gulielma Springett in 1672. In 1910 additions were made to the building and it was renamed King John's Farm.

The courtyard of King John's Farm, showing the original building and part of the 1910 extensions. Compare the timber-work of the building on the right with the photograph of the original house (above).

King John's Farm. The external balcony and stairs were part of the 1910 additions, but were removed sometime in the 1930s.

The front of King John's Farm, 1920. Apart from the trees and shrubs, the view is almost the same today.

Looking across Lower Road to South Road in the early 1920s. This photograph clearly illustrates the number of houses that had been built by then, and the unmade-up state of the road.

Christ Church and the common in the 1920s. This photograph was taken during the improvements to the main road.

Quickley Lane looking towards Stag Lane school, just visible on the skyline in the distance, in the 1920s.

The Cedars, *c.* 1910. At this time it was a private house. It was built in the late eighteenth century for Mr J. Gilliatt MP, and after the First World War it was purchased by Mr Henry Batty who gave it to The National Institute for the Blind, who converted it to a school for blind girls. The school closed in the 1980s and the building is now the centre of a retirement homes complex.

This happy family group was photographed in 1934 in Berry Lane, between Chorleywood and Mill End. The author is on the right, with his younger brother, mother and uncle.

Youngers Retreat, Chorleywood Bottom, *c.* 1910. The road leading to the common can be seen on the left, leading past a cottage called The Retreat, which is still there today.

Two views of Shire Lane in the early 1920s. Above: looking down Blacketts Hill, with the railway arch at the bottom. Below: looking in the opposite direction, with Haddon Road on the left.

Chorleywood, photographed from the common in the early years of this century, when there were only a few houses to be seen in South Road. The railway can be seen running across the centre.

The junction of Station Approach and Common Road in the 1950s, before extensive alterations were made.

MILL END AND
WEST HYDE

Uxbridge Road, Mill End, in the 1920s. The Tannery House is still there today. In the distance can be seen the chimney of the old Mill End Mill. This was one of a series of photographs taken by Mr Andrews, a local shopkeeper, who reproduced them as postcards for sale in his shop.

Grove Road, Mill End, in the early 1920s. It is very different today – the road has been made up and cars are parked along both sides of it.

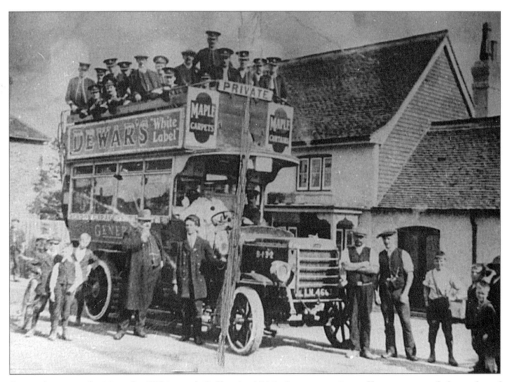

A coach outing leaving the Whip and Collar in 1916. It was setting off on a tour of the pubs of Rickmansworth and Croxley Green on the day before the new licensing laws were brought in restricting pub opening hours.

Uxbridge Road near Church Lane in the 1920s.

The same scene as above but taken from the opposite direction in the 1960s. The gable-ended buildings had been turned into shops by that time; they have all since been demolished and the site is now occupied by Mill End Garage and a block of flats.

The Tree public house on the corner of Church Lane and Uxbridge Road, *c.* 1910. The pub itself is still there, but the walls have been refaced and both the tree and the cottages beyond have gone. It was originally called the Rose and Crown. The name was changed about the time of this postcard; hence the two names on it.

The opposite corner of the same road junction as shown above, *c.* 1910. The Vine public house, the buildings next to it and those on the other side of the road have all been demolished, but the ones on the right in the distance are still there.

Church Lane, Mill End, in the 1960s. These cottages were demolished to make way for the Clarkfield development of houses and flats.

A note on the back of this 1912 photograph describes the two men as 'gravel diggers in Mill End Pit', but unfortunately does not give their names.

The original water pumping station in Uxbridge Road which was opened in 1888. The buildings were demolished in 1966 and replaced by the present ones which stand on the site of the original wells.

This quiet scene is the Uxbridge Road, c. 1912. Long Lane Farmhouse can be seen in the distance. The Red House on the left, the farmhouse itself and all the trees have now gone, and today this is a very different scene.

May Cottage, West Fyde, 1920. This is one of the oldest buildings in the area and dates from the early seventeenth century. The people are believed to be Jack and Doris Davis.

These very plain Victorian cottages which stood on the Uxbridge Road next to the Tree public house were photographed in the 1960s. The site today is the wide verge opposite Mill End Garage.

This old watercress bed lay to the west of the old road at West Hyde, and was built as an extension to the branch of the canal which came to Troy Mill. In the 1960s it was filled in and today no trace of it remains.

The Royal Exchange Cottages at West Hyde stood on the old road near the junction with Chalfont Lane. In the 1960s, shortly after this photograph was taken, they were demolished and replaced with new houses.

Shepherds Farm in Middleton Road, Mill End. It was demolished in the 1960s to make way for the Express Dairy's bottling plant, which has in turn been demolished and houses now stand on the site. This house was the home of the Lane family in the seventeeth century. In 1642 it was owned by George Lane and three of his sons, Job, James and Edward, who left to seek their fortunes in America and settled in Massachusetts. There is no record of Edward but the descendants of Job and James often visit this area looking for this house.

Mr Stevens (right) with his van behind his shop in Uxbridge Road. The Mill End Garage now occupies the site of the shop.

Money Hill House, Money Hill. Most people will remember it as the York House School for boys, now located at Red Heath, Croxley Green. The Meresworth retirement homes stand on the site today.

Local workmen laying some of the first gas mains in Mill End, 1928.

The footpath beside the millstream behind Uxbridge Road in the 1920s. A new footbridge crosses the stream at this point today opposite the Tyre Services depot, and trees have grown up on the left bank, but the houses shown are unchanged.

The Grand Junction Canal at Springwell Lock, 1910. On the left is the River Colne, which flows under the towpath to join the canal at this point.

This rural view was photographed from the hillside near Springwell Lane in 1902, and shows the canal in the foreground, the River Colne on the left, and Uxbridge Road in the distance.

The Narrows in Uxbridge Road, *c.* 1910. It looks very different from the busy open road that it is today. All the cottages and buildings shown here have been demolished over the years. The gateway on the right was the entrance to Mill End Mill, and today there are some shops on the site, behind which can be seen the millstream and a few traces of the mill race.

The old infants school in Church Lane, photographed in the 1920s. It closed as a school in the early 1970s, and in 1976 it was taken over by the Mill End Community Association who still occupy it today.

Council workmen carrying out road repairs in Church Lane in 1939. The ground behind the fence on the bank is today the site of the parade of shops.

BATCHWORTH AND THE CANAL

The locks at Batchworth, c. 1920. This is one of the best-known views of the canal. It was taken from Church Street bridge and it shows the main canal on the right and the local branch on the left. This branch is the canalized River Chess which runs over a weir next to the lock and joins the River Colne a few hundred yards downstream.

The old White Bear pub, 1909. Mr and Mrs Mayo are nearest to the camera.

The old White Bear public house at Batchworth in 1913, shortly before it was due to be demolished. The landlord Mr Mayo and his daughter Kathleen can be seen in the doorway.

The rear of the old White Bear pub photographed during demolition in 1914.

The new White Bear public house, photographed in 1914, shortly after it reopened. This is the present building. In the doorway are Mr and Mrs Mayo and their daughter Kathleen.

This photograph of Batchworth was taken in 1910 by Mr T. Price from the top of the chimney of Batchworth Mill which was being demolished at that time. The White Bear is at the bottom left, the old Batchworth bridge over the River Colne is in the middle. The course of the River Colne can clearly be seen crossing the canal, and Bury lake is in the distance.

London Road, Batchworth, in 1910, when the millstream was the open waterway shown here, with the mill on the far left. Today the stream lies under the waterworks garden, all the buildings shown have gone and the road is a dual carriageway.

London Road, Batchworth, looking in the opposite direction. The White Bear and Batchworth bridge are clearly shown.

This well-known postcard shows the demolition of Batchworth Mill in 1910. The building on the left was not demolished and still stands today as part of the waterworks complex.

This view of Batchworth Hill is believed to date from coronation day in 1911, as the people are standing in the road in their best clothes, and there is a marquee in the garden on the left.

An outing from the White Bear in 1909. The occasion is not known, but it seems to be something special as Mr Mayo, second from the left, looks as if he is making a toast with a wine glass in his hand.

A group of children attracted by a barrel organ outside the White Bear in 1909. Unfortunately the name of the organist is not known but the lady sitting down with the cat is Mrs Mayo.

A summer's day on the River Colne at Batchworth in 1914. The piles of bricks in the background were probably being used for the reconstruction of the White Bear.

A postcard view of Harefield Road in the 1920s. It is impossible now to pinpoint the exact location.

Batchworth Heath from the London Road looking along White Hill, 1910. The cottages shown here survived and are still occupied today.

The lower entrance to Moor Park Mansion in Moor Lane in 1902. It is no longer there. The main entrance was from Batchworth Heath.

A busy scene at Walker's boat-building yard at Frogmore Wharf on the canal, *c.* 1910. Tesco's new store stands on the site today.

This photograph of the canal at Batchworth, looking towards the Church Street bridge, perfectly captures the peaceful atmosphere of 1902. The stables on the left were destroyed in a fire in the 1950s, but part of the floor (which has dated bricks in it) can still be seen today. The buildings on the other side have been demolished, and the Trinity Court office complex stands on the site today.

Mr and Mrs Mayo and their daughter Kathleen in the garden of the White Bear public house, 1914.

A canal family caught by the camera passing through the area in the 1950s. Although the boats seemed to be very overcrowded, these people always seemed to be happy.

PEOPLE AND PERSONALITIES

This 1907 postcard shows Lady Ebury presenting prizes at a local flower show. Lord and Lady Ebury lived at Moor Park Mansion and were great benefactors to the local community, supporting local events and giving land to the townspeople.

Miss Edith Price (left) and her sister Flori in Rickmansworth Park, 1900. Their father owned the newsagent's shop in Station Road, where he had been in business since about 1890. Edith took many of the photos in this book which date from 1900 to 1914. In 1909 she married a widower, Thomas Mayo, the innkeeper at the White Bear at Batchworth. She appears with him in some of the photographs taken at or near the pub. Their daughter Kathleen, later Mrs Bowen, is the lady whose generosity has allowed us access to Edith's wonderful collection of photographs.

In 1943 HRH The Duchess of Kent paid a visit to Croxley Mills; she is seen here with the manager, Mr A. Bone.

The recreation ground at Ebury Road was officially opened by Lord Ebury in 1911, on land which had been given by him to the town. The man facing the crowd in this photograph is believed to be Mr A. Freeman, the council surveyor.

'Ye Old Fogies of Rickmansworth' were a group of local businessmen who got together for a good time, and incidentally raised money for charities and other local good causes. Mr Bob Walker is at the front left, and Mr Thomas Mayo is at the front right.

This group photograph was taken at the Rickmansworth Cricket Club in Park Road when the club-house was opened in 1924.

To our right good & trusty friends

Miss E. Price

GREETING.

Ye Old Fogies of Rickmansworth

purpose to hold their ancient revels on ye eve of Wednesday ye
23rd March, 1904, at ye

Town Hall, Rickmansworth,

where ye are bid to join them for a right good time of song and
dance. Ye will be welcomed at 8 of the eve and farewells and
good wishes bid at 3 o' the clock of ye early morn.

We pray thee friends that ye tarry not
But send your hearty answer right early.

This 'Old Fogies' invitation card was sent to Miss Edith Price by Mr Thomas Mayo in 1904. It certainly sounded as if it would be a good party. Thomas married Edith in 1909.

A group of children at Parsonage Road School in 1916. Two of the boys, Ernie Harris and Sid Phillips, are still alive today.

The Price family from Station Road enjoying a Sunday stroll in 1900. They are shown on the footbridge over the River Colne in Caravan Lane. In the background is the bare Metropolitan Railway embankment, which had only been in existence for thirteen years at this time.

A Sunday school outing, *c.* 1900; second from the left in the back row is the Reverend Fisk.

SHOPS AND BUSINESSES

Wrights Garage in Park Road in the 1960s. This photograph clearly shows the 1930s style of the building, the canopy and the petrol pumps. The canopy was damaged in 1990 and in 1991 it was demolished and the petrol pumps removed, and the whole of the front of the building had a complete facelift in the style of the new Vauxhall Masterfit Service.

Wrights Garage in the late 1920s. Wrights Motors is the oldest established business in the town: it was started in 1920 when Mr Harry Wright, the father of the present owners, started a haulage business working from the yard of the Feathers public house. He moved to the present site in 1922, and by the 1930s the company was operating a fleet of eighteen heavy lorries and running a general garage. The building shown here was built in 1912 and is still there today, forming the basis of the present showroom and service bay.

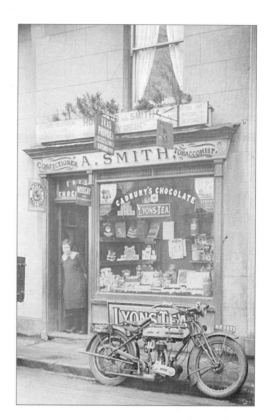

Smith's was a small general store on the Uxbridge Road near the Halfway House, situated in the row of cottages called Two Stones. The shop front can still be seen today.

Bone's shop in the High Street will be remembered because of the great variety of items it stocked, and the fact that many of them were displayed on the pavement! Marks and Spencer stands on this site today.

Pullen's shop on the corner of Solebridge Lane, Chorleywood, in the early 1900s. The signs high on the wall state that it was the first post and telegraph office in the area. Although it has changed hands, it is still trading under the same name today.

This drawing is one of the few illustrations we have of Loudwater Mill showing how it looked in the late nineteenth century. The mill has been demolished but the house shown is Glen Chess which is still there today.

Tyler's, one of the best-known shoe shops in the town photographed in the 1920s. In 1965 the building was demolished but the shop resumed trading under the same name in one of the new shops built on the site.

One of the oldest family businesses in the town still owned by one family is Dickins' wine merchants. This photograph shows the premises in the early 1960s when it was a general grocers, and shows the founder Mr Frank Dickins with his son Roger on the bike.

The Victoria Hotel opposite the Metropolitan Line station, *c.* 1900. The advertisement across the bottom of the photograph was painted on the wall bordering Rectory Road. The hotel is still there today but is now called the Long Island Exchange.

The water company's directors' car in the 1920s. The driver was Mr H. White, who also drove the company's steam traction engine.

An unusual sight in Rickmansworth High Street in the 1920s: a Tasker 'Little Giant' steam tractor, complete with police escort, tows a wide barge from Walkers' yard in Harefield Road to Springwell for use in the gravel pits there.

Scotsbridge Mill in the late nineteenth century. The exact date of these buildings is not known, but there is a record of a paper mill here in 1757. It continued to produce paper until 1885 when it was forced to close because it was polluting the river. It then had various owners and uses; it served as the headquarters of MGM Pictures from 1939 until the 1970s. Then, after being left empty for a number of years, it was purchased by the Beefeater restaurant chain in 1988 and turned into the restaurant that it is today.

Scotsbridge Mill in the 1960s. The white outbuilding is now the site of the porch and front entrance of the restaurant.

Mr Stevens in front of his shop in Uxbridge Road in the 1920s. The building has since been demolished and Mill End Garage stands on the site today.

Tesco's first shop in Rickmansworth in 1936. It stood on the corner of Station Road and the High Street. Note that there were already traffic lights on this corner at that time. Tesco have moved a number of times in the town since the 1940s. First they moved across the road in the High Street and then to Penn Place. In 1992 they moved out of the town centre to their new superstore in Harefield Road, built on the site of Walkers' timber yard.

Bury Restaurant, 1965. This house stood in Bury Lane next to the Bury Garage. The restaurant closed in 1965.

The Rickmansworth picture house as drawn by Edward Paget-Tomlinson. This was the first purpose-built cinema in the town and opened on 12 March 1927 at the east end of the High Street. It continued in business until 22 June 1963; the town's other cinema having already closed in 1957. The building has now been converted into offices.

The Zerny Engineering Company started business in these premises in Church Street in 1952, the year this photograph was taken. They are still in business today but are now located around the corner in Norfolk Road. This building is now an office.

The van in this 1926 photograph belonged to Warner's family butchers who had a shop in the High Street. The man on the left is the author's father, Mr E.C. Parrott.

PARADES AND
CELEBRATIONS

The Young Conservatives' float in the Rickmansworth Week procession in 1959. This is now an established event in the local calendar; it was started in 1955 and is still going strong. Many of the young people shown here still live in the area.

These two photographs show the 1911 coronation procession in the west end of the High Street. The 'giant' was Tom Newton who owned the shop on Batchworth bridge.

This lorry was the water company's contribution to the coronation procession in Rickmansworth in 1937. The men shown all worked for the company; they are, left to right, Mr Early, Mr Crosby and Mr Harris.

United Charities parade, August 1915. This parade toured the area, taking nearly all day, to raise money for two local wartime emergency hospitals, one in St Augustin's Hall, the other in Mount Pleasant Studio.

A church parade, 1 August 1920. The parade is coming down Station Road and is seen here just before the road turns under the bridge. Almost every society seemed to have banners in those days, which they loved to bring out on almost any occasion; the one at the front represents the National Union of General Workers, Kensal Green branch.

These two photographs were taken at the Station Road corner during the coronation procession on 16 July 1902. It is not clear exactly what route the procession took as in the photograph above it is turning right into the west end of the High Street, with another float waiting to join it, but in the photograph below it is turning left into the central High Street.

This splendid family photograph was taken outside the greengrocers shop on the corner of Talbot Road and Church Street, probably during the Jubilee celebrations of 1935.

The coronation decorations in Church Street, as seen from the corner of the High Street on a quiet Sunday morning in 1902.

A view towards the railway bridge at the east end of the High Street on the same quiet Sunday morning. The large building on the left was demolished in the 1930s and was replaced with the 1930s-style one which can be seen there today.

Another view on the same quiet Sunday morning in 1902: the only things moving in Church Street are two dogs. The Chequers pub is on the right.

The same Sunday morning again, this time in the High Street looking towards Church Street corner.

The funeral of Mr W.H. Gill, the Superintendent of Works for the Rickmansworth and Uxbridge Valley Water Company. The coffin was carried on a company trailer drawn by the company's steam traction engine, driven by Mr H. White. It is shown here coming round the corner towards Batchworth bridge in November 1930.

This photograph of the west end of the High Street captures the atmosphere of the 1937 coronation procession, with one of Wright's lorries providing the float for a club from Mill End. It looks a bit risky as the men appear to be vaulting on the moving lorry, and notice how close some of them are standing to the back of it!

Another view of the coronation procession at the corner of Station Road. This photograph and others of this occasion were taken by Edith Price from the first-floor window of her father's shop in Station Road.

The 1902 coronation procession coming down Station Road. This is another of Edith Price's photographs.

A Sunday school procession in 1912, probably on Whit Sunday, at the bottom of Scots Hill. The young girl in the dark dress with the white frill (bottom, centre), is Edith Newton. Also on display are a number of society banners; the first one represents the Independent Order of Oddfellows.

A sports day on the Fortune Common at the bottom of Scots Hill. It is believed that this photograph dates from 1902 and the event was part of the coronation celebrations. Pictured is the finish of a one-mile flat race.

The Gravel Bashers Band forming up outside the Whip and Collar public house in Uxbridge Road, *c.* 1910.

The dedication of the war memorial in the grounds of St Thomas's Church, West Hyde, on 2 May 1920. Although West Hyde has always been part of Rickmansworth, it became an ecclesiastical parish on 3 November 1846 and therefore has its own war memorial.

SOME WARTIME MEMORIES

Four of Wright's lorries drawn up on the Rickmansworth bypass in 1945. They were shortly to leave for France, together with their drivers, to distribute food and other supplies after the liberation. Imagine the fuss if they tried to take a similar photograph today on such a busy main road!

In 1939 one of Wright's lorries was requisitioned by the British Army who took it to France. It was abandoned at Dunkirk where it was found by the German Army, who modified the chassis before using it. After D-Day it was recaptured by the RAF who used it for a while before it was finally brought home. The company, not realizing its potential historic interest, put it back in service, eventually disposing of it when the fleet was modernized. It is shown here being refurbished in 1946 after being returned to Wright's.

This Second World War pill-box can still be seen on the bank of the canal at Stockers Farm. A series of these structures were built in this area and, together with the canal, they formed part of the outer ring of defences for London in 1940.

These railway lines embedded in the ground on the approach to the canal bridge at Stockers Farm are part of the 1941 anti-tank defences; they can still be seen there today.

This 1940 pill-box in the field off Tolpits Lane is one of the largest built in this area.

An air-raid siren was put up on the waterworks building at Mill End. Like all the others in this area it was only removed in 1994.

During the Second World War, from 1940 onwards, members of the Women's Land Army were employed by Walker's at Frogmoor Wharf. Some of them are shown here parading up Station Road.

Some of the soldiers and nurses at the auxiliary hospital which was set up at Chorleywood during the First World War.

MISCELLANEOUS

This was the scene at Rickmansworth station on 9 September 1961 when the last steam train to be used on this line made a special journey to Amersham. In 1926 the line from Baker Street to Rickmansworth was electrified, but since the trains went to Aylesbury this meant that the engines had to be changed at Rickmansworth. By 1961 the line had been electrified as far as Amersham which then became the terminus. At the same time the old-style carriages seen here were replaced by the tube-style trains which are still in use today.

An aerial view of Moor Park Mansion, taken in the 1970s.

The Artists Rest Home at Mount Pleasant in 1963 being demolished to make way for the Penn Place development. The house on the right was also demolished at this time.

This photograph of Rickmansworth was also taken from the top of Batchworth Mill's chimney in 1910 (see page 68). The canal is in the foreground, with the Gasworks Arm running across the centre and the railway beyond that.

In the early hours of the morning of 17 March 1947 parts of Rickmansworth were hit by a flash-flood. This was the scene in Church Street. The water drained away the same day and since then work on the river banks has ensured there has never been a recurrence.

The original wooden railway station at Church Street dated from the opening of the railway in 1862. It was demolished in 1921 and replaced with the brick structure shown below.

The depressing scene at the deserted Church Street station in 1966 before the lines were lifted; nature had already started to take over. It was finally demolished in 1973.

WATFORD AND RICKMANSWORTH RAILWAY.

THE LORD EBURY, CHAIRMAN.

PROGRAMME

OF PROCEEDINGS ON THE OCCASION OF THE

TURNING OF THE FIRST SOD

OF THE RAILWAY

AT RICKMANSWORTH

BY

THE LORD EBURY,

ON THURSDAY, NOVEMBER 22nd, 1860.

The Company will assemble at the Watford Lodge of Moor Park at 12.30, where they will be directed to the site of the intended Ceremony, which will be marked by Flags, &c.

On the Bugle call, the several parties invited to witness the Ceremony will proceed to take their places.

The Engineer Mr. J. S. Peirce, will address Lord Ebury and request the honor of his TURNING THE FIRST SOD of the *Watford and Rickmansworth Railway*, and will present his Lordship with the plans and particulars of the Line.

His Lordship will then proceed to turn the first Sod, &c.

The Rev. A. H. Barker, Vicar of Rickmansworth, will ask a Blessing of the ALMIGHTY upon the work.

His Lordship will express his thanks and those of his brother Directors to the several distinguished visitors for their attendance, and invite them to a *Déjeuner.*

Three Cheers will be given for the QUEEN.

The Band will play the *National Anthem.*

Three Cheers for Lord Ebury, and for the success of the undertaking.

The Band will then march to the National School Rooms, RICKMANSWORTH, playing " *Oh, the Roast Beef of Old England.*"

A handbill advertising the 'turning of the first sod' ceremony for the Watford and Rickmansworth railway.

Moor Park Mansion, in the 1920s. This Grade 1 listed building was built in 1678/9 by James Duke of Monmouth. In 1720, when Benjamin Styles was the owner, the original house was faced with Portland stone and the magnificent portico was added to the front. The house is often seen on television. National golf tournaments are held in the grounds, and the house has also been used as the setting for a number of period films.

Croxley Green station shortly after it was opened in 1925. It is still virtually unchanged, and is a fine example of a building of the period.

Looking towards the goods yard at Church Street station in the early 1950s; at this time it was still in use. St Mary's Church is visible on the right.

The opening of Rickmansworth fire station in the High Street, 2 September 1891. The building is still there, but today it houses a fish and chip shop. The plaque set in the wall by the door bears the names of some of the first firemen; it is also still there. Note the unmade-up state of the road, and the lack of pavements.

A once-familiar scene at Rickmansworth station: an electric locomotive waiting in 'The Dock Road'. This engine was no. 7, *Edmunde Burke*.

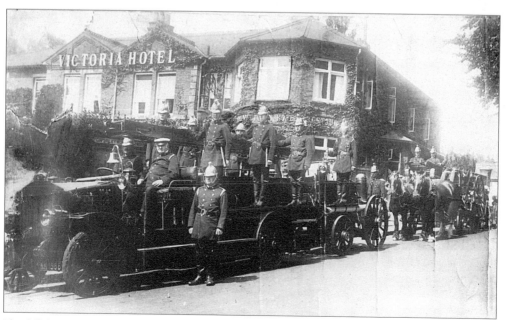

The full fire brigade drawn up outside the Victoria Hotel. The date is not known but it must be after 1921, when the first vehicle in the picture, a Pearce Arrow ex-war pump, was purchased.

The original fire brigade, photographed in full fire-fighting dress, on their first manual pump. The brigade was started by Dr Henderson in 1861 and most of the volunteers were local tradesmen.

An accident on Scots Hill, 13 April 1912. A traction engine towing three trailers ran away and overturned.

The construction of the M25 viaduct in Berry Lane woods, where it crosses the Metropolitan railway. Built in October 1974, this viaduct received an award as one of the best concrete structures of the year.

ACKNOWLEDGEMENTS

Copies or originals of all the photographs reproduced in this book can be found in the files of the Three Rivers Museum. Thanks are due to the large number of people who generously donated their photographs to the museum, or loaned them for copies to be made. It is impossible to name all the individuals, and if people see their photographs here I hope they will understand.

I would especially like to thank the committee of the Three Rivers Museum Trust for permission to use photographs from their files, and the following people or organisations for their photographs or help in various ways:

Wrights Motors • *Watford Observer* • Tony Walker • Rickmansworth Historical Society
The Godfrey Cornwall Collection • M.R.F. and R.E. Tame • Mr and Mrs L. DeWaay
Mrs K. Bowen

Finally, I would like to state that all the historical information in the captions has been checked as far as possible, and is believed to be correct. However, it should be regarded as no more than a guide to the best information available to me at this time.

To order any of these titles please telephone our distributor, Littlehampton Book Services on 01903 72159(
For a catalogue of these and our other titles please ring Regina Schinner on 01453 731114